Vicious Verses and Reanimated Rhymes

edited
by
A.P. Fuchs

COSCOM ENTERTAINMENT
WINNIPEG

COSCOM ENTERTAINMENT
130 Stanier Street
Winnipeg, MB R2L 1N3 Canada

This book is a work of fiction. Names, characters, places and events either are products of the author's imagination or are used fictitiously. Any resemblance to actual events or persons living or dead or living dead is purely coincidental.

ISBN 978-1-897217-95-5

All poems contained herein are Copyright © 2009 by their respective authors. All rights reserved, including the right to reproduce in whole or in part in any form or medium.

PUBLISHED BY COSCOM ENTERTAINMENT
www.coscomentertainment.com
Text set in Garamond
Printed and bound in the USA
COVER ART BY SEAN SIMMANS
EDITED BY A.P. FUCHS

Library and Archives Canada Cataloguing in Publication

    Vicious verses and reanimated rhymes : zany zombie poetry for the undead
head / edited by A.P. Fuchs.

ISBN 978-1-897217-95-5

    1. Zombies--Poetry. 2. American poetry--21st century. 3. Canadian poetry
(English)--21st century. I. Fuchs, A. P. (Adam Peter), 1980-

PN6110.H67V58 2009   811'.6080375   C2009-902221-4

VISCERA

Isabella by Adam Huber 1
I, Zambi by Kyle Hemmings 4
Forever by Charles A. Gramlich 6
Narcissus, Deceased by Steve Rasnic Tem 8
Undead Valentine by J.H. Hobson 9
Love in the Time of Zombification by C.J. Lines 10
The Zombie Blues by Paul A. Freeman 13
Forest Lament by Michael Josef 14
The Zombie Flu by Janet L. Hetherington 15
Sudden Death by Lester Smith 17
The Virus by Sheri Gambino 18
Dead Land by Keith Gouveia 20
Don't Zombie Me by Chris Bartholomew 21
You Are Horror and Light by John Philip Johnson 23
Zombie Zombie by Robert M. Hildebrand Jr. 24
Twenty Questions by Gregory L. Norris 25
Zombie Love by Paul A. Freeman 27
Discourse of a Zombie by Mercedes M. Yardley 28
Me Returneth by W. Bill Czolgosz 30
My Zombie Journal by Matt Betts 31
County Morgue by Greg Schwartz 34
Natural Succession by Chris Lynch 35
Reanimation by Casey Quinn 36
5 Dark Ravens by Joseph Grant 37
A Re-birth by Robert Essig 38
Amore, Zombie Style by Lin Neiswender 39
Misfire by Mark Webb 40
Dead Poetry Jam by J. Bradley 41
One Plus One Equals Yum by J.H. Hobson 43
Zombie Bride by Jonathan Pinnock 44
Romero Bouquet by Zed Zefram 45
Last Year by Michael Kriesel 46
Her Box-song, Unending by Alex Dally MacFarlane 47
On the Outskirts of the Last City of the Living by Kevin James Miller 48
Zombie Slave by John R. Platt 49

Grandpa by Michael Cieslak	50
Death Shall Not Part by Ronnie K. Stephens	51
The Call of the Corpse by Gayle Arrowood	52
We Suffer! by Robert Essig	54
Zombie at My Door by John Hayes	55
Necromancin' by Kevin Lucia	56
A Day in the Death of a Zombie by Carla Girtman	58
The Maintenance of Certain Standards by Rachel Green	60
State of Emergency by Eric Ian Steele	61
Decay by Carl Hose	62
Say Cheese by Albert Melear	63
Echoes of Identity by John R. Platt	64
What They Want to Tell Us, But Can't by C. Hildebrand	65
Zombie Lovers by Sheri Gambino	66
Teeth by Casey Quinn	67
Evolution of the Dead by Sheldon S. Higdon	68
Show and Tell by James S. Dorr	69
The Burning Zombie Question by Shaula Evans	70
Former Vocations by Aaron Polson	71
Institutions of Higher Learning by Zombie Zak	74
Bed and Breakfast by Joe Nazare	76
Feast by J. Bradley	77
Crème Brûlée by Katherine Sanger	79
Caroline by Eric Ian Steele	80
Canned Beans by Greg Schwartz	81
Incarnate by Jennifer Williams	82
Sapid by Adam J. Whitlatch	83
Slow Bites by Steve Vernon	84
It's Never Too Late by Roxanne Fuchs	86
Preparing for the Eventuality by Stephen D. Rogers	87
Them by Eric Ian Steele	88
The End is Come by Zombie Zak	89
A Zombie Sestina: Only Flesh by Tonia Brown	90
Invidia by Jennifer Williams	92
Such a Little Thing by Camille Alexa	93
Corpse by Michael Cieslak	96
They Eat Our Brains by J.C. Hay	97
Oh, Scheherazade by J.P. Wickwire	98
Surviving the Horde by Peggy Christie	100
The Living, the Dead, and the Entropic by Eric Hermanson	101

The World Has Gone to Hell by Zombie Zak 103
Esurient by Adam J. Whitlatch 105
Cold, Dead Meat by C.A. Young 106
Zombie Love Sonnet by Anthony Watson 107
When the Dead Were Among Us by Kara Ferguson 108
Git Along, You Zombies by Lester Smith 110
Trapped by Sheri Gambino 111
Kismet by Adam J. Whitlatch 112
Rage, Rage in the Dying of Twilight by Rich Ristow 113
The Hunger by Susan Satterfield 114
The Whites of Their Eyes by Andrew J. Wilson 115
Zombie Weather by Michael Kriesel 117
Born to Death by Mark M. Johnson 118
The Day of Re-birth by Sheri Gambino 119
Morte D'Amour by Jennifer Williams 121
Head Out by Nathalie Boisard-Beudin 122
Zombie Semi-Sonnet by J.H. Hobson 124
Fred by Berrien C. Henderson 125
Devolvement by Ginger Nielsen 126
Deadly Relationships by Patsy Collins 127
Zombie Attack Escape Plan by Claire Askew 129
Payback Time by Paul A. Freeman 131

Vicious Verses and Reanimated Rhymes

ISABELLA
by Adam Huber

The bile
      Drip
            Drip
      Drips from her distended jaw.
She hovers above me
And I cry
This was never supposed to be.
My throat clenches
      And hers
            It flexes.

Before it all started she was someone else.
We all were:
      Me—a father
      Her—my daughter.
The roles have changed:
      Her—the hunter
      Me—the prey.

Her eyes are glossed over,
Empty,
Instinct at its most primal.
And she
      My Isabella,
            Is surging with raw hunger.

The officials, they tried to explain,
      They gave reasons,
But there's nothing
      That can truly explain the horror
When your daughter is a beast.
      There are no reasons.

The smell of rot is strong.
Isabella is salivating in streams.
She lunges and bites.
My tears aren't from the pain;
    Spill and mix
        Blood and saline.
It's all come to a head.

Nothing more than an object
    Of blind rage;
It was her mother who killed her.
Since the virus,
    Family has meant everything
        And nothing,
Depending on your side of death.

I am nothing,
    Not to her,
    Not any more.
Her teeth are dull,
    But she's quick and strong now.
        Whatever she's become makes her mouth hot on my flesh,
            A fever like she had during a bout with chicken pox.
I should fight,
    But I don't,
        Can't.
She's my Isabella
And she hasn't won.
    So much as I've lost,
    So much as we've all lost.

The spread was rapid
    But we were careful.
Isolated.
It was a stray dog that did us in:
My wife,
My daughter,
Now me.

As my throat tears
  And her blunt teeth crush my windpipe,
    I'm thinking of the swing set in the backyard.
We built it together,
  The weekend before her sixth birthday,
    Three years ago now.
And I'm wondering if she remembers,
But her eyes remain blank,
My blood staining her mouth and chin.
There's the smile
  That got me through so much,
    Now tarnished and tweaked and twisted.

I'm slipping
  And my greatest fear
    Even above the pain
Is a gnawing thought:
When I come back
  Will I remember?
Will she still be my Isabella?

I, ZAMBI

by
Kyle Hemmings

At our stately mansion over Twin Moon Hill
Paid with my wife's generous dowry,
I labored in the cellar lab
From morning to night.
It smelled of moss and sulfuric fumes.
I was trying to invent a recipe
To cure the world of its ills,
Its diseases and bad tempers,
But I pushed this agenda aside.
My wife was growing cold,
No longer so easily offered herself to me
In the old sense.

I suspected affairs and midnight debaucheries.
I sensed the ghosts of other men in our bedroom.
It was only weeks before that I had my brother,
Such an impressionable and fragile bachelor,
Committed for insanity.
At night he would howl like a wolf.
The doctors claimed that love drove him mad.
But what love was this?
For the moment, my wife was my only priority.

In the lab, filled with specimens from all over the world,
I searched for a solvent.
I searched for a solution.
With rubber gloves I collected the secretions
Of a bouga toad, then added the detrotoxin
From a puffer fish.
I mixed tarantulas and millipedes,
The seeds of poisonous plants,
The skins from tree frogs

And ground-up bones.
The recipe for making a zombie.

In the parlor, I sidled up to my love,
Who was reading a book on the virtue of chasteness.
I rubbed the brew on her skin and kissed her soft cheek.
Soon, her skin appeared blanched and her eyes froze.
She keeled over—very much a dead woman.
But not for long.
I then applied the potion known as "zombie's cucumber."
Within minutes, as my fingers shook,
She opened her eyes and slowly rose from the floor.
But she could not speak nor remember who she was.
I had robbed her of both personality and soul.

I led her into the bedroom and commanded her to undress.
In bed, planting frugal kisses on her face and neck,
I knew it was her who had driven my brother mad.
And outside, the wind cried, *I, Zambi.*
Or was it a wolf?

Or perhaps I was just hearing things.

FOREVER
by
Charles A. Gramlich

At the dawn these soldiers rise
From the fields where bitterness lies.
Blue and gray, wide eyed with fear
They gird their loins for battle here
To fight, to kill, for all they hold dear.

And so with weapons grim to hand,
With throats carved sharp with cries,
They strike the music, the martial band,
The cannons sing, the grapeshot flies.
They loose the fateful battle hound,
They charge upon the red, red ground

And death it comes, they fall like sheaves
Of wheat and corn, or like winter leaves.
The ragged lines, they bow and bend,
The smoke across the land does wend
And the broken only God can mend.

But across the way they come on bold,
Like the mythic heroes of old.
They will not turn, they will not break,
Beneath the sun whose rays do rake,
They will not, their flag forsake.

And from the pall their enemies loom,
The bullets whisper, sweep like a broom.
The charge it carries to the lines
Through the carnage, through the mines.
Hand to hand with foes they grapple
And with gore the fields do dapple.

Whisper/screams of doubt and pain
Roil and echo across the plain.
The men they fall to move no more
For the queen of war, that faithless whore.

Then night descends to cloak the dead
Where these soldiers now are bled.
Silence paints the scarlet ways
Till sun and soldiers both arise
Forever through the weary days
Gettysburg, they do reprise.

NARCISSUS, DECEASED
by
Steve Rasnic Tem

In the dirtied mirror
That's your face, your lips,
Your eyes like cameras
For the real you thousands
Of miles or years away.
You raise your old hand
On thirty-second delay, try
To caress yourself, but only
Paw with ruptured fingers
Like make-up sticks; smear
The liquid you through
Ruined terrain. That's you,
This destination you weren't
Meant to see. Open
Your flappy lips, push out
That bloodless tongue. Your attempt
To choke yourself never
Works. The mouth hangs
Ready, but the howl
You push with everything left
Never arrives.

UNDEAD VALENTINE
by
J.H. Hobson

Oh let me bite your lips, my dear,
You will thank me, never fear.
You'll be undead just like me,
Eating brains eternally!
Say you love me, say you will
Stay with me undead until
The last warm brain has been digested
And all zombies are conquested

LOVE IN THE TIME OF ZOMBIFICATION

by

C.J. Lines

I'd told Marlene I'd be back soon—"I'll only stay for one,"
But that was several beers ago and now I'm having fun.
It's nearly half-eleven and I'm pondering a gin
When the pub doors fling wide open and some layabouts lope in.

There's three of them in total and they don't look very well,
Their skin is pale and crusty; they emit a ripened smell.
They're staggering and stumbling as though they're slightly tipsy.
I nudge the barman, leaning in, and say, "Perhaps they're gypsies?"

He bellows, "Sorry, gents, but I'm afraid you missed last orders."
He's hoping that will be enough to dispel these marauders.
They don't appear to understand and lurch in my direction.
A clammy hand goes for my throat—my final recollection.

When I come to, I'm on the floor; the clock says half past three.
Marlene is going to flip her lid—I'll get the third degree.
It's then I look down and see that my neck's been ripped to shreds,
A gaping hole is pumping out my blood all down my threads.

The barman's slumped against the wall; I think he must be resting,
Until I notice, pouring from his gut, are his intestines.
It's strange, although I'm injured, that I can't feel any pains.
I try to call out for assistance but can only gargle, "BRAAAAINS!"

The barman hollers back at me and struggles to his feet,
But soon he topples forward as more innards he excretes.
I realize that I must get home and tell Marlene I'm mauled,
For surely she'll assist me and the police can then be called.

I fall into my car outside, drip blood upon the seat,
My stomach starts to rumble; I've a craving for some meat.
I start the motor, floor the gas and swerve along the road.
I see a lone pedestrian and he's very swiftly mowed

I slam the brakes and tumble out; I pounce the warm cadaver.
I bite, I chew, I rip out flesh, my hands with blood are slathered.
I gulp his brain, the sweetest part, I swallow, then I belch.
I rummage through his insides with a slosh, a splash, a squelch.

My hunger's briefly satisfied, my head's a little clearer.
I get back in the car and then discretely check the mirror.
My skin is peeled and rotten and my teeth have pointy tips,
My eyes are dark and bloodshot and there's blood all down my lips.

I shrug still feeling nothing and continue homeward bound,
But Marlene's locked the door and so I have to howl and pound.
Eventually, she answers it and I try to crack a grin.
She shrieks in abject horror, slams the door and hides within.

Her attitude is saddening, but I won't be disparaged.
I fumble with my keys awhile—I'll get in through the garage.
I'm having trouble with the lock and somehow snap a finger.
I throw the digit on the floor—I've got no time to linger.

Eventually I get inside and shamble through the hall.
Marlene is on the carpet; she's all curled up in a ball.
She yells, "Just keep away from me! I'll call the freakin' cops!"
I lunge towards her for a kiss and out my eyeball drops.

I pay no heed, just watch it as it rolls towards the den.
I try to say, "I love you" but it sounds like "BRAAAAINS!" again.
I grab her face and kiss her and I hope it's understandable.
I bite too hard; when I pull back, off comes her lower mandible!

I chew it a little in my mouth and I'm drooling blood.
Her eyes roll back into her head. She crumples with a thud.
I nibble on her ankles while she lays there for a while.
Ten minutes pass, then suddenly she wakes and tries to smile.

It's hard for her to talk; her mouth makes incoherent sound.
"BRAAAINS?" I ask her gently and her head nods up and down.
We both rise from the carpet, feeling hungry for new flavours.
I point towards next door—it's time for dinner with the neighbours.

THE ZOMBIE BLUES
(A LIMERICK)
by
Paul A. Freeman

An elderly zombie named Fred
Was excited at being undead.
But losing his dentures
Upset his adventures,
Then bunions confined him to bed.

FOREST LAMENT
by
Michael Josef

He leans against the tree,
Hand and head on its trunk,
Searching for the beat
No longer in his own heart,
Wondering if he should stay motionless
Like this giant.
Reach his arms up to the sky
Like branches,
Stretching toward a heaven
That will no longer welcome him;
Dig his toes into the earth and take root
Alongside these trees,
His brothers,
Who also live with no breath,
No heart.
Let the world keep moving on its axis
Toward its own fate
Of blood,
And death,
And rot.
The tears he wants to shed,
Like his own death,
Will never come.
Something moves nearby,
Brought to the ground by its own momentum.
Tripping on the roots of his kin,
This new entity looks up at him and screams.
Tears are no feat for it.
He can hear its heart beating a song,
And can smell the bouquet of fear and sweat
As it gets up to run.
Into the forest of his brothers,
He leaves his place by the great tree and follows.

THE ZOMBIE FLU
by
Janet L. Hetherington

"My, my, you're very pale,"
They said at work, so I
Took some time
To shake this flu
To spend at home
To cozy up
And rosy up
My sallow skin.

"I can't explain this cough,"
The doctor said, so he
Wrote a note
So I could spend
More time at home
And take some pills
To cure the ills
That make blood thin.

"You want to eat it raw?"
The waitress asked, then she
Gave the bag
With take-away
To eat at home
Sanguine attar
Of steak tartare
To sink teeth in.

"You're looking at me strange,"
My lover said, then I
Staggered up
And lumbered to
Employ embrace,

Heart beating full
Of dreams of skull
And brains within.

"Just shoot it in the head!"
The marksman cried, as he
Raised his gun
And pointed it
To hit straight home,
And as I fell
I heard him yell
Of bested sin.

"My, my, you're very pale,"
They said today, as I
Could only stare
From my new home.
My coffin closed
I lay in state
So wide awake
And so done in.

SUDDEN DEATH

by
Lester Smith

They rose that night from Lakelawn Cemetery.
The frozen earth in which they were interred
could not hold them. As a mob they entered
the rink, where skaters drilled in symmetry.
Zombies are slow, and certainly no faster
on ice. Reduced to an ungainly crawl,
they lurched like crippled colts in a corral.
Necrotic flesh, with wounds all full of fester,
stuck to the ice like tongues to frigid metal.
The hockey team had padding for protection,
and skates and sticks to chop through putrefaction.
That night the hockey players proved their mettle!
Then, after they'd dismembered every zombie,
the scraps played havoc with the team's Zamboni.

THE VIRUS
by
Sheri Gambino

I am here to infect you.
Once I enter your body there's nothing you can do.
What am I, you ask?
A zombie virus so lethal, killing you is my task.
Creeping in through a fresh cut,
I enter your blood and stay very quiet.
Coursing into your bloodstream,
I multiply and develop my killing team.
Now it is we that will start to eat.
To us you are nothing but tender meat.
You start to feel the ache;
Fever rising you start to shake.
Yes, that is it, lay down in bed;
Entering your brain, soon you'll be dead.
We are eating you alive;
Thriving and continuing to multiply.
Your guts and organs fulfill our needs.
Blood clots start to proceed.
You cry out in pain;
We are eating your brain.
Blood oozes from your eyes.
They dilate to full size.
Your body starts to expand,
Shaking all over, trying to pull up by your hands.
Clenching teeth, they start to crack;
Convulsions throw you back.
Pressure becoming more intense,
Body functions becoming dense.
It's time for the big pop;
As you explode your heart stops.
Blood and guts spurt everywhere.

Now our seeds fly in the air.
Out of the house we glide,
Now blowing through the sky.
We wait for you to breathe.
Entering, infecting, with our seeds,
Our numbers will grow over night.
Humans will die and come back to life.
Zombies will now walk the streets.
We're looking for you to eat.

DEAD LAND

by
Keith Gouveia

I am a slave to the hunger,
No less a victim than those I kill.
Its voraciousness drives me, consumes me,
Mocks me as I devour all I once held dear.

But now there's nothing left to eat.
The streets are devoid of movement, save my own.
It's inevitable: mankind will soon be extinct
Like the dinosaur, nothing left but bones.

In time, the Earth will heal for a new master.
But what, I ponder,
Will rise out of the rot to claim our throne?
I am so hungry.

How long has it been since my last meal?
The hunger is unbearable.
Only meat can satisfy the pain.
Fresh, rotten, it all tastes the same.

I look to my arm to see the maggots.
They, too, are dead, and gorge on my flesh,
The skin gray with rot, but I realize,
There's still enough meat for one last meal.

DON'T ZOMBIE ME
by
Chris Bartholomew

My family was gone, of that I was sure,
My friends where nowhere to be found.
I ran and ran, stopping only when safe,
Temporary, no place was secure.

I made it to the store, but as I walked out
I saw all the bobble-heads making their way.
I stopped and held hands with a mannequin
Perfectly still, but wanting to scream and shout.

In the commotion of people running and being eaten,
I and the mannequin were knocked down.
She lost a leg and her head in the fall;
I tried to stay sill, sure I'd be found.

When the last slobber and tendon tear was heard
I waited, paralyzed, filled with fear and great dread
As the dead men went walking . . . away

On my way out I slipped on
Intestines, bloody feet and a pair of ears,
Headed to a nearby station not frequented
A placed hidden amongst spare parts and gears.

Nothing prepared me for the night, the horrid sounds,
Screaming, the squish and pop of ripping flesh, bones.
Slow scuffling footsteps passing on the street now;
The tormented are silenced, tormentors search the grounds.

With everyone gone survival is truly the key
Yet with everyone gone, what is the point?
Where will I go and what will I do
If no one is with me?

The survival instinct tells me to get up and run,
To run and find other people to help them survive.
How many bodies of decay will I have to visit before
I give out and give up, knowing it's the end of some?

YOU ARE HORROR AND LIGHT

by

John Philip Johnson

Before you wanted to kill us all the time,
Things were better, back when we were like siblings.
You, the normal older brother, with a soft spot
For us, your retarded kin. Except even then
You couldn't hide your distaste for us.
Something about our staggering gait,
Our blind stare, our groping outstretched arms
You didn't like. Maybe our decaying flesh
Made your skin crawl, and the thought
Of what we do on Saturday nights
Was too much for your gentle sensibilities.
Maybe our astounding strength threatened your ego,
Or our relentless plodding insulted your sense of purpose.
Mother Theresa among the lepers you were not.
Plus, we got a hankering to eat your brains,
Did I mention that? But what should we eat?
Dogs? Dandelions? What else in this abandoned,
Black universe is there for the undead to eat except
The gray, wet joy of your brains? When the unholy sun
Climbs into the sky like a boil swelling with pus,
The light scalding us and burning out our eyes,
You are the light, you are the terror we hunger for.
You are the destroyer, the monster, the one
We tell our rotted little children about,
The horror that hides at the heart of all things,
Our deepest hunger, the fount of light, living
And blooming, outpouring from your brains.

ZOMBIE ZOMBIE
by
Robert M. Hildebrand Jr.

Zombie zombie burning bright,
I sit and watch your head ignite.
Your screams, they give me an awful fright.
Oh zombie zombie burning bright
Your friends begin to gather round
And pull out marshmallows;
You wear a frown.
The flames they leap from the top of your head,
And so you wish you were truly dead.
Oh zombie zombie burning bright.
Stop, and let me get a light.

TWENTY QUESTIONS
by
Gregory L. Norris

What if late one afternoon the world ended; not quickly in clouds of fire, but slowly, painfully, with teeth, one angry bite at a time?

What if in a twist of cosmic irony the Earth, left with no other choice, chose to recycle us?

What if you were driving home from work in that usual, afternoon fugue, not really living so much as going through the motions; in limbo because life, until you heard the news screamed over the radio, had long ago lost its meaning? What if one diseased corpse became two, the two four, and so on? The dead walk!

What if in less than two weeks' time the living were outnumbered?

What if you and your husband James survived the first wave that killed the cities and civilization's gadgets, and you found yourselves hiding in an attic room at the dawn of a modern stone age, in a terrifying new world?

What if your food and water supplies ran dangerously low while the creeping silence steadily drove you insane? There is no radio, satellite or otherwise, because there is no power. And it's not like you'd dare listen, for fear you might be found out. There isn't much in the way of conversation, only hushed whispers. No cable TV. No high-speed internet, no latest hip-hop or oldest classical to break the monotony, only the ghostly howl of the wind, the occasional dragging footstep, a scream from somewhere in the night. The quiet is deafening.

What if, instead of the old luxuries like the big house and expensive car, all you wanted were the basics—a hot meal, a hotter bath, a solid night's sleep without jolting awake, a shriek lodged in your throat? What if, while staring out at the colorless, rain-lashed landscape, you realized those blessings were things of the past, that there was no room for bubble baths and freshly-baked bread in this reality?

What if one morning you glanced into James's eyes and saw them driven mad with hunger, fear?

What if the scrubby apple tree growing at the periphery of your line of sight, visible through the attic window, called to you in a siren's voice?

What if, each armed with weapons, you crept down the stairs, aware of the danger, aware of each croaking footstep, but too starved to care?

What if, for the first time in weeks, you dared step outside, through the backdoor, into this dead new world?

What if you made it to the apple tree, but the world wasn't as dead as you hoped?

What if you swung the baseball bat, weak from days of inactivity and lack of food, but driven giddy by the desire for revenge?

What if one of the corpses bit James in the meat of his shoulder, right at the armpit?

What if you made it back inside the house, but only now they knew you were there? You heard them tromping around downstairs for days and nights on end—dozens maybe *hundreds*—all wanting their pound of flesh.

And what if you awoke to find James icy to the touch, cold following days of fever from his infected bite wound, and he looked at you with those amazing blue eyes, only now they were the eyes of a stranger, rheumy and rabid? And like so many clueless survivors the world over, so many sheep, you assumed this lump of flesh and teeth and disease was still the person you loved and hesitated from driving the nearby ax into its skull and, instead, mistook that curl on its lips for a smile, an invitation for a morning kiss, and you leaned closer, closer yet?

What if?

ZOMBIE LOVE
by Paul A. Freeman

Shall I compare thee to a hunk of meat
Hung out all day beneath a summer's sun
To fester in the fetid, fly-blown heat?
Your reek doth more my rotting nostrils stun.
Though autumn winds break off limbs of trees
As those unzombied folk might sever ours,
If you're un-armed, my eyes you shall please,
Like meadows strewn with multicolored flowers.
Upon the uninfected shall we feast;
We'll swallow down their choicest, gory cuts.
And if they dare to call you "fiend" or "beast"
I'll reach inside them, ripping out their guts.
So long as I can shuffle in the streets,
I'll fetch for you hosts of bloody treats.

DISCOURSE OF A ZOMBIE
by
Mercedes M. Yardley

Listen,
He tells me.
I try not to stare at
The brown flesh
Stuck in his teeth.

It's not like he has a choice,
At least,
Not anymore

He waves his hands around as
He talks,
Wiping his mouth across
His rotted arm.

At one point, sure,
Maybe,
I would have said,
"No way, man,
Not me.
I'm not this,
A scavenger, a parasite.
I'm so much more."

He sucks on somebody else's fingers,
Gnaws on somebody else's marrow,
Then drops their knuckle joints
Into a delicate glass bowl.

But that's the way things work:
You get into something so deep,
Become somebody that you never thought

You'd be,
And suddenly you find yourself.

He stops, his eyes shiny.
I had bitten my lip so hard it bleeds.

"You gonna eat that?"
He asks.

ME RETURNETH
by
W. Bill Czolgosz

Arrrghh.
Luhhrrrr.
Ingh.
Vuuhhh.
Ecchh.

Arrghhh.
Grrruhhh.
Arrrr.
Inngghhh.
Nuuhhh . . .

MY ZOMBIE JOURNAL
by
Matt Betts

Day 1

This isn't so
bad. Took me forever
to walk to the
post office, though.
Wish I were one
of those fast zombies
like in the movies.

I wonder if that
guy on the lawn
is dead or sleeping?

Day 2

Turns out the guy
on the lawn
was dead. Took brains.
So hungry. Wandered along
with some other
zombies toward
the mall for a while.

Seemed like
a stupid idea. Who would
hide at the mall?

Day 3

Down brains the river
I brains some
people hiding on a
boat. They waved and
taunted me with
their brains. Mmmm.
Sea food.

Sadly, I
discovered I can't
swim anymore.

Brains 5

Brains in brains
brains
brains brains the brains
others won't
share brains
with the brains
of us.

Stupid brains
making me
brains even more.

Day 6

Floated into
a city filled
with brains.
Some guy shot me
twice. I ate him.
It was great. Not so
hungry anymore.

I think better on
a full stomach.

Day 21

I know I had
two
arms when I came
into this town
but I seem
to have left one
somewhere.

Ah well,
dude with the
chainsaw was tasty.

Day 28

Started walking
down the highway
toward the capitol.
Ran into a
group of zombies all
chanting,
"Spleens, Spleens."

You really
find some weirdos out
in the suburbs.

COUNTY MORGUE
by
Greg Schwartz

County morgue,
The corpses give the coroner
An autopsy.

NATURAL SUCCESSION
by Chris Lynch

The zombie is an ecosystem:
Worms and bugs and lizards, even a snake
Burrow from the hungry birds that cling
To rotten shoulders as it lurches;
A travelling sideshow
Of freaks.
Bright spiders spin their webs oblivious
In face ferns and the unfurling fig tree,
Catching moths, mating like monsters
While the bird-borne strangler, green seducer,
In suburban silence sucks the human flesh
And grows.
That gardener's head now encased in wood,
A cage of secret lives and sudden deaths—
Yet still the whole thing hunts for blood;
The rootless wanderer has not one
But many greedy mouths
To feed.

REANIMATION
by
Casey Quinn

Shoot 'em
In the head
Is what she said.

When I turned
To look
It was too late.

She was
Already dead.

But then I blinked
And wouldn't you know,

She was standing there
Yet
Again.

5 DARK RAVENS

by
Joseph Grant

5 Dark ravens sitting on a power line
While other birds are singing pretty verses.
They are cawing funereal morning curses,
Their black, empty empathy is mine.

5 Dark hearts conspiring against my own,
Kisses from the grave, embraces from the gloom.
Death of love inside the wedding tomb,
Their love sucks the marrow from my bone.

5 Dark girls wanting nothing but my money.
For that, their bodies they give to me.
They have abandoned love for misery
As my mind worms with their own VD.

5 Dark souls writing depressing verse,
Adorned in black, rejecting all salvation,
Embracing the abject resurrection,
Divorced from life, for better or for worse.

5 Dark thoughts fly from my head;
5 ominous vows as Death my wife I wed;
5 former virgins as I rise from my funeral bed;
5 thoughts of rhyme carry me to the edge;
5 dark paces as I step off the ledge.

A RE-BIRTH
by
Robert Essig

The breath of life re-enters
Those asleep in the graveyard.
Pain as muscles stiffen beyond rigor mortis
Enter the infancy of life beyond death.
Hands like leather-wrapped bones
Dig through rotten coffin-wood and dirt,
Blindly searching for
A second chance, a re-birth.

Bony hands break through the earth's crust
From so many graves like grim flowers.
Corpses emerge, rotten and groaning,
Clumsily searching for salvation.
Bodies stiff, every movement as painful
As their re-birth into damnation.
There is a hunger, deep and fathomless;
Only human reckoning can suffice.

Loved ones come back from the grave,
With loveless minds fueled by primal instinct.
It grabs your face with fingers poised;
Tears a morsel of your being.
You try to flee but cannot move
As teeth sink in, life you lose.
Your eyes re-open to see a new light.
Damned with the pain of human blight.

AMORE, ZOMBIE STYLE
by
Lin Neiswender

How do I love thee?

Let my body count the ways.

Your warm embrace
Makes this zombie's heart race.
Baby, let's go eat some brains.

Your fingers may rot
But I'm still besot;
Smell of putrid flesh attracts me.

Your knees may wobble
But I still hobble
Toward you on one foot and a skateboard.

Your heart is still
Yet gives me a thrill
When I see it poking out your ribcage.

Your eye so bright,
Lost the other one last night
In a scuffle with a rival clan.

Your dragging arms
Another of your charms—
Come, gimme a kiss.

But I forget—no lips.

MISFIRE

by
Mark Webb

Dark, thick fingers of smoke stretch for supplication to the sky
As I lay *st*-staring with my one good eye.
Fire heat creeps from the downed chopper to meet me.
I look to my right and see what used to be Sam, my co-pilot, now a charred husk.
He—*it*—is slumped over the melted throttle.
Hungry . . .
Flashes of *mem*-memory assault me.
Fl-flying over the creek, scouting for the two missing girls.
Hungry . . . so hungry . . .
Hovering too low. Clipping a *tr*-treetop and losing control.
Plummeting. Explosion. Blackout.
Slowly, I get to my feet.
Rise . . .
Fire . . . get away . . .
My legs are like lead. My gait-*walk* . . . is unsteady.
So hungry . . . must eat . . .
Pain . . . then no pain . . .
I stumble through the brush—*look for food*—follow the sound of the rippling creek
As the sound of the water increases—*new smell*—I begin to notice voices.
My legs move faster, though still stiffly, almost as if by their own will.
Closer . . .
Branches claw at my face but there is no pain.
Can smell it . . .
Hungry . . .
I break through the bushes to see—
Food . . .
The two girls *pl*-playing in the water.
They look at me . . .
Food scream . . .

DEAD POETRY JAM
by
J. Bradley

We never . . . asked to be . . .
Rotting wrecks . . . shuffling
Here . . . there . . . wherever
There may be . . . flesh . . .

We were . . . humans once . . .
Just like you . . . except the throw . . .
Of the dice . . . landed on snake eyes . . .
The black dots . . . much like the teeth marks . . .
On what's left . . . of our arms . . . or our sides . . .

Others . . . infected by viruses . . .
The ones that walk . . . are the ones that survived . . .
They move fast . . . like clichéd lightning . . .
And the thunder . . . the screams . . . of the living
Gnawed . . . to a bloody pulp . . .

Some of us . . . can articulate . . .
Learned to hide . . . slivers of humanity . . .
In our bloated . . . cheeks . . . the hollow caverns . . .
Where our intestines . . . once were . . .

Please . . . put your shotguns away . . .
I come not to eat . . . but with something . . .
To say . . .

We . . . the undead . . . are tired
Of how scared . . . you become . . . when we . . .
Saunter towards you . . . arms extended . . .
We just . . . want some comfort . . . a hug . . .
Consolation . . . over our fate . . .

The problem . . . with fighting . . . zombification . . .
Thoughts derailed . . . by choruses of hunger . . .
I look at you . . . and I see a menu . . .
I'd smack myself . . . but then I might . . .
Lose an ear . . . or two . . .

We tire . . . of your mistreatment . . .
Your oppression . . . of our kind . . .
Wait . . . I meant *I* . . . or did I . . .
No . . . I meant *we* . . . as in us . . .
As in me and my . . . fellow zombies . . .
We tire . . . of you . . . not treating us . . .
As equals . . . just because we like . . .
To eat . . . people . . .

We deserve . . . to live . . . just like . . .
You . . .

That's right . . . raise your shotguns . . .
Threaten us . . . with your weed whackers . . .
Your propane tanks . . . your school busses . . .
Retrofitted with . . . chainsaws . . .
And steel planks . . . you may mulch us . . .
Mutilate us . . . dye your clothes . . .
With our blood . . . but we will keep coming . . .
Oh yes . . . we will keep coming . . .

Wait . . . I'm sorry . . . I didn't mean . . .
To sound threatening . . . you try
Resisting . . . becoming the walking undead . . .

Stop this madness . . . stop killing us . . .
Stop treating us . . . as less . . . than human . . .
Because . . . if you don't . . . we will get really angry . . .
And really . . . hungry . . .

And to show you . . . how serious . . . we are . . .
I'll be eating . . . your friend . . . and your wife . . .
And your kids . . . and you . . . and you . . .
And you . . . and especially . . . you . . .

ONE PLUS ONE EQUALS YUM
by
J.H. Hobson

An undead math teacher went back
To school on a surprise attack.
The head of his class
Was a brainy young lass
Whose gray matter made a great snack.

ZOMBIE BRIDE
by Jonathan Pinnock

Everyone's talking about depression,
Credit crunch and world recession,
But I'm still feeling warm inside,
'Cos tomorrow I marry my zombie bride.

It's true her lips aren't made for kissing
(The top one's there, the bottom one's missing)
But she's my girl, we'll never part—
Quite literally, I have her heart.

I want to hold her, I want to thrill her,
I want to give her some necrophilia.
Ashes to ashes, dust to dust,
I'm overwhelmed with zombie lust.

There'll be no family at the church—
Both sides have left us in the lurch.
They were aghast to hear our news,
Like the Capulets and the Montagues.

But I don't care, I know it's love.
She's my undead angel from above.
I had to woo her, I had to win her—
Hope she doesn't want me for dinner.

ROMERO BOUQUET
by
Zed Zefram

Roses are red
Zombies are gray
They'll come after you
Either night, dawn or day

LAST YEAR
by
Michael Kriesel

Purple tulips
Zombie fingers poke
Through melting snow

In the corn
Scarecrow wanders
Zombie crows don't fly

Army on TV
I shoot
The moaning wind

Zombie summer
Everyone wears
An orange hat

Zombie girl chained
In a basement
Music starts upstairs

Trick or treaters
Tell real zombies
By the smell

Lincoln's statue
Students chant
Zombie rights!

Christmas sale
White ashes
Land on shoppers

HER BOX-SONG, UNENDING

by

Alex Dally MacFarlane

I sing from subterranean rocks,
Perched and eager in the dirt
With skin hanging from my head
Like hair: blood-scented hanks
Still tainted by formaldehyde.
I cannot soil-scrub it away.
In rectangular boxes, hip-wide,
I am reminded of roses,
Lavender and carnations—
The girl-smells of my hair
Before it fell out—and I
Tear open the sides, feeling the rot
Of old petals, old clothes
And skin like soft pillows for my face.
Here, too, I find chemicals,
But they peel away under
My scissor-bone fingers
And deep inside are only
The smells of her, girl-beautiful:
Slipping so sweetly down
My throat-remains. Too quickly
I scrape fingers against an
Empty dish. Always too soon,
Always. Out I must crawl
In a dirt-shimmy I perfected
Long ago, sidewise pushing
Through dirt and roots, boxes
And rocks: I find one, lichens
Faded dead yet clinging still.
I perch, eager-poised, and sing
For the next box plunged down,
Hoping it will come soon.

ON THE OUTSKIRTS OF THE LAST CITY OF THE LIVING

by

Kevin James Miller

Dead, you know me better now than when we both lived.
Living, I never found my courage.
Living, it vanished with my morning coffee and yogurt.
Living, I put on each day's dress and went to the office.
Living, but the invisible woman.
Living, the world and I awoke one day to Alpha-69.
Living, it ravaged, authored by some government, any government.
Living, maybe ours, frightened of the future, the world, us.
Living, maybe finally scared of itself.
Living, whatever creator it was, of the ultimate murder weapon.
Living, billions, but then dead.
Dead, but then after a while, re-awakened.
Living? No, dead, I among countless others.
Dead, but animated non-living to only hunt and devour
The living.
And living, you were one of dozens of men who ignored me.
Living, trying to, you ignored me, you more than most.
Living, dead, what did it matter to me?
Living, dead, enough loneliness and anger erases all boundaries.
Dead, those who had been generals were scared boys.
Dead, but animate, but having lost the power of life.
Living, I knew nothing of power.
Dead, I took it and now take it every day.
Dead and dead stand beside me my love, as me and my armies stand here
On the outskirts of the Last city of the living
Ready to complete the job of slavery, conquest
And dinner.

ZOMBIE SLAVE
by John R. Platt

**Congratulations!
You have just created
Your very own
ZOMBIE SLAVE!**

Just remember,
While quite amenable,
Zombie slaves will not:

- ✓ Do the dishes
- ✓ Wash your windows
- ✓ Finish your homework
- ✓ Lie to telemarketers
- ✓ Fix your roof
- ✓ Do your grocery shopping
- ✓ Play bass in your band
- ✓ Scare off the paperboy
- ✓ Tell your mom you're not home
- ✓ Spy on your wife
- ✓ Organize your comic book collection
- ✓ Hook up your TiVo
- ✓ Wait in line for you at the DMV
- ✓ Do your taxes
- ✓ Or change the litter box

All else is fair game.

GRANDPA
by
Michael Cieslak

Blue-green algae spread across a cheek.
Once the landing place of thousands of tiny kisses.
Milkly blank stare, these windows to the soul,
Forever shuttered, eyes which had once looked upon
Every act as a miraculous accomplishment.
Lips blackened, rotted through, teeth
Which once smiled
Now bared;
Grimace not grin,
Closer, ever closer,
Leaning in, not to praise nor kiss,
But to bite.

DEATH SHALL NOT PART
by
Ronnie K. Stephens

The chill of her icy corpse
Rouses me from closed-casket rest.
Decay-gray skin sticks to mine.

Crimson stalactites ooze life's
Liquid into my mouth, desire stinging
Tongue's tip. Raven hunger hollows,
Bone-white fingers shred my back.

Her bleeding scent burns my throat.
I sink molars into her flesh but vein beds
Are cracked and dry. Lift chapped sex lips
To mine, suck greedy for lust wine. Nothing.

Ghoulish howl erupts, echoes off her
Starved cavern walls. Pledge of eternity
Mocks souls caged in long-buried bodies.

Yellow nails pierce soft soil,
Digging through uprooted turf.
Beware of resurrected lovers.

Graves cannot entomb desire.
It is time to feed.

THE CALL OF THE CORPSE
by
Gayle Arrowood

Come get us. Come get us.
Don't ignore the stench.
Hurry! Get us soon.

We're loaded in ditches
Ten people high
Beside dirt mountain roads.
Our beds of stone stick to our bones
And villains go unhung.
They leave us, they forget us.
Hear us, hear us, now's the time.

Come get us. Come get us.
Don't ignore the stench.
Hurry! Get us soon.

We're burning under the desert sun,
Buried all but our heads,
And all of us in a long, long bed.
We scream and screech
When the buzzards come to call,
But on our heads, they caw
And drop their drippings.

Come get us. Come get us.
Don't ignore the stench.
Hurry! Get us soon.

We're drowning in the deep
Of river, lake and sea.
Trawlers for us. Trawlers.
We'll rise to your arms

In whole or in parts.
We need to find eternal rest
Nestled in the breast of the earth.

Come get us. Come get us.
Don't ignore the stench.
Hurry! We'll get you soon.

WE SUFFER!
by Robert Essig

Night air cold on my aching bones.
Eyes burning toward misshapen figures.
Body moving robotically in agony.
I taste copper on my cracked lips.
There's a churning in my brain
Of maggots living therein.

I smell you.
      Your blood!
      Your life!
I hear you.
      Your movements!
      Your breaths!

Frenzied, I seek your flesh,
A shape in my cataract eyes.
My body dances with a pulse
Of maggots disintegrating my being.
My wretchedness is upon you now.
My hands clasp and you scream.

I feel you.
      You squirm!
      You thrash!
I taste you.
      Your flesh!
      Your blood!

Now you are as I am.
We suffer!

ZOMBIE AT MY DOOR
by
John Hayes

Lightning streaks against my window.
I hear the squeal of my front door.
A zombie motions from the stoop,
"Come, Archibald, my master awaits your presence."

I shove the zombie;
He staggers back.
I slam and bolt my door,
Load five bullets in my revolver,
Hug it beneath my pillow
And sleep a restless sleep.

Next night arrives and when lightning streaks
I hear the squeal of my front door.
The zombie motions from the stoop,
"Archibald, my master awaits your presence."

I fire three shots into his body;
He falls, then rises.
"Come, Archibald, our master waits no more."

I fire a shot into his mouth;
Pain spreads upon my tongue.
He laughs, removes spent cartridge from my mouth,
"Come, Archibald, I guide you to your fate."

I shoot into his eye;
Pain scorches in my vision
He laughs,
Removes spent cartridge from my blinded eye,
Twists me toward the enigmatic night.
"Come, Archibald, your master waits no more."

NECROMANCIN'
by
Kevin Lucia

Do ye know what's about
When corpses leap an' shout,
When they runnin' through the fields
An' all their wounds're healed?

Hot visions burn their eyes
Of lands lost in time
When their hearts beat in line
Fer women who were fine.

Do ye ken what's about
When c'davers clamber out,
From soil moist an' deep
But their souls they don' keep?

They leap fer the sky,
Grabbin' all that they spy,
Be it yours, be it mine,
Ever sure they'll never die.

Do ya hate what ya see
When the pale come 'n' eat,
Smirk 'n' smile through their teeth
As on yer flesh they feast?

From the gutters they will rise,
An' the places where they died
An' they can never hide
From the stink behin' their eyes.

Necromancin' is the game,
For all those seekin' fame,
Who wanna raise the dead,
From their damp an' earthen bed.

But beware voodoo's guile,
For ever all the while
Yer heart grows malign,
An' black it swells in time.

Till one day at yer best,
It explodes in yer chest,
An' suddenly yer dead,
With dark fancies in yer head.

An' when the moon is risin' high
While the worms eat yer eyes,
Ya stumble an' ya moan,
Wet shadows now yer home.

Now ya do all the same,
An' eat the flesh of black shame,
While ya feed on the lame
'Cause Necromancin' is the game.

A DAY IN THE DEATH OF A ZOMBIE
by
Carla Girtman

Lost a finger, lost my toes,
Walking's hard; zombies know.
Near the door, in shadow waiting.

Need some brains to feed the madness.

My days are numbered; I know this fact.
But I'll face death when sinews snap
And dissolve into goo.

Experiments are for losers who die anyway.

Must be sly, must be clever.
Knee gives out; tendons sever.
Time's running out for me.

I hear the truck. Dinner's coming.

Bat in hand, ready to swing,
Key in door, the phone rings.
Strength is fading fast.

My swinging bat spills brains.

Body quivers, body shakes,
Scoop the brains onto a plate.
Tongue slobbers round my dinner.

Buzzing madness fades.

Muscles soften, sinews melt,
Final breath, relief is felt,
Releasing madness in a viscous flow.

The hourglass has turned. Time is up.

THE MAINTENANCE OF CERTAIN STANDARDS

by
Rachel Green

One has to keep up
A pretence of civility
Despite one's uncouth neighbours.
No gorging of soft tissues
Or internal organs
Or dining in the street where your victim fell
Screaming obscenities through the blood
Bubbling in her throat,
Choking the words until her sobs fade
Into pleas and half-remembered prayers.
Hilda and I prefer our meat
Medium rare—just a hint of pink,
If you please,
And would you drain the blood?
Ribs in the oven.
Half rack or a whole one, dear,
And what about the head?
Poor Mr. Granger.
He was so upset when you ate his dog
And that was before you turned.
Neighbourhood cook-outs
Were never the same after that.
When the virus came
You knocked on his door
And said you were sorry
As you bit out his throat.
The cheek
Is tasty.

STATE OF EMERGENCY
by
Eric Ian Steele

They told us it was all under control,
Then when that failed, to pray to save our souls,
When the fires started and the hungry screams
Of those who died began to haunt our dreams.

"Don't panic!" came the old familiar cry.
Now panic's all we have since reason fled.
We live from day to day, from place to place,
Hoping never to see another face.

Nobody ever told us why or how
Death came along that night wielding his plow.
But not content to chop them down like grain,
He came and dug the dead ones up again.

Is there no room in Hell that dead men walk?
Perhaps if those infected lips could talk
They'd tell us death is not the greatest fear,
But that we made our Hell on Earth right here.

DECAY
by
Carl Hose

I see through dead eyes
The way they look at me.
I must look a mess;
A sight to see.
Flesh hanging from bones,
My teeth rotted away;
A walking corpse
In full decay.
Grave dirt smudges left behind
As I amble on my way;
I leave behind the smell of death,
The stench of living decay.

SAY CHEESE
by
Albert Melear

Pump-action shotgun
White-knuckle gripped in my hand;
I pull the trigger,
Spraying a mist of zombie
Innards all over the wall.

ECHOES OF IDENTITY
by
John R. Platt

Skin loose
Shambling, stumbling
Reaching, rending
Mindless
Flies buzz, feast
Rotting flesh
     Teeth so sharp

Dead-alive
Shadow
Echoes of identity
Falling away
Not what you once
Were

Need, hunger, desire, thirst
Unquenchable
Eat drink tear consume
     No satisfaction

Always craving
More, more, more

Feed me

Join us

WHAT THEY WANT TO TELL US, BUT CAN'T, BECAUSE THEY'RE ZOMBIES

by
C. Hildebrand

What they don't tell you
Is that they feel
Like marshmallows.

And,
What they don't tell you,
Is that to them,
We smell like
Graham crackers
Or chocolate.

And,
What they want to know is:
Why would anyone
Not want to be a s'more?

ZOMBIE LOVERS
by Sheri Gambino

Zombie love, what a beautiful thing.
Two dead people in love, once human beings.
Holding hands and ready to eat,
Looking for fresh human meat.
Milky eyes gaze for prey,
Spotting a human, it is their lucky day.
Working together as a team,
Staring at each other with a lustful gleam.
Stumbling quietly, not making a sound,
They unlock hands, ready to pounce.
Grabbing the human with their hands,
Biting into his flesh as hard as they can.
The meat bag was screaming, trying to break free;
Biting into his neck, tearing out his throat,
Blood splashed everywhere as he choked.
Sucking and slurping out the man's eyes,
His mouth was open when he died.
Zombie lovers continued to eat,
Entrails hanging out of their mouths,
Blood covered bodies that stunk of fowl.
Leaning over, touching lips,
Exchanging food with a kiss.
Eating every morsel with slurping groans,
Sucked him dry, nothing left but bones.
Zombie lovers rose to an upright stand,
Walking away, holding hands.

TEETH
by Casey Quinn

Teeth flossed and
Brushed for decades,

Strengthened with
Each chomp
Into an apple,

And jaws
Grown strong
From tearing
At the fleshy
Steaks and ribs
Off the grill
On a hot
Summer night.

Teeth prepared
Perfectly

As if
We always knew

They could
Be used

As a weapon.

EVOLUTION OF THE DEAD
by
Sheldon S. Higdon

Clawing up from their graves in sixty-eight,
An unsuspecting farmhouse lies in wait.
The departed led by their appetite,
A cemetery visit begins the night.

A shot to the head kills the dead.
A shot to the head kills the innocent.

Walking in an endless sleep, they consume;
Registers cease to ring a happy tune.
Holed up in the mall with their weapons drawn,
Gangs infiltrate, must survive till dawn.

A shot to the head kills the dead.
A shot to the head kills the infected.

An experiment of a gentle kind,
Decayed memories slowly come to mind.
Everyday items used to be the way;
An undead revolution brings the day.

A shot to the head kills the dead.
A shot to the head kills the living dead.

SHOW AND TELL
by
James S. Dorr

Hear the tap-tapping,
The death-beetle's knock,
A bone crashing on coffin-wood,
Flesh and rot bouncing.
The gas causes this, they say,
Decomposition,
The corpse decay's function—
The body will twist, they say;
Meat shrinks from fingernails,
Skin puckers under hair—
All part of nature
As, cadavers rising,
Death makes its own answer.

THE BURNING ZOMBIE QUESTION
by
Shaula Evans

No one talks about zombie poo
But you never see them queue for the loo.

FORMER VOCATIONS
by
Aaron Polson

I.

Something is rotten in my garden.
It was once a man;
his name dangles from
a broken tag on a torn shirt,
a green shirt
from the organic grocery
on the corner.
A vegetarian,
perhaps a vegan?
But now, *it*
shambles in gray impatience,
snapping its broken-toothed jaw,
dripping strings of
pestilent saliva,
groaning for
the meat
on my bones.

II.

Last summer,
the man brought an audience to
their feet, roaring
for Mark Antony's revenge—
but the plague
let loose the
dogs of war,
the once-human watchers
of his theatrical game;
his friends, his neighbors, his audience,

fell upon him
chomping and snatching
at scraps of his skin,
rending and tearing
as if to take inside
some bit of the words
he brought to life.

III.

When she taught third grade,
the fence was to keep
the children in,
and she filled their
hungry brains.
Now, she is the worm's concubine;
her fingers
drape the chain-links,
her flesh hangs in
loose strips,
her eyes
milked-over with cataracts
as she hungers for the
little ones.
But she—*it*—
is on the outside
and the hunger
is different.
Insatiable.
Foul.
Only *slowed* by the fence,
never stopping.

Never stopping.

IV.

Walled in her basement studio,
blind eyes staring—
a sort of painter's block.

Before, when they surprised her at the sink,
the freshly-rinsed brushes
made poor defense
against jaws and fingernails.
Now she gnaws on the canvas,
Pthalo blue smears with
dried brown of human blood.
Too stupid to work the doorknob
with hands torn off at the wrist,
she flails and flails.
Her fluids strike the walls,
an homage to Jackson Pollack.

V.

Old and worn-out.
Retired.
He sat in the rocker on his wide porch,
watching
the first waves stumble and spill
down the street—
a monster of a mob,
all hands and teeth.
Too tired or slow,
he watched them break neighbors' windows.
Deaf, he barely heard their cries
(the railroad took his ears).
He muttered through the dentures,
(he never said much, anyway).
Sans ears, sans teeth,
he still had eyes
to watch as they shambled up his steps
and took the rest of him
in gulping bites.

INSTITUTIONS OF HIGHER LEARNING
by Zombie Zak

We at the Institute of Higher Zombie Learning
Are always at the pinnacle of life's open yearning.
The brittle caprice to which the living blunder
Speaks volumes at which we, the dead, wonder.

"How is it that a species such as this rhyme
Continues to exist and thrives in this clime?
To breed and spread their values as they are
From the nearer close to the absolute far?"

These are the questions that the Zombie Horde
Whisper amongst the shadows in dark discord.
We swallow the secrets that Life has to offer
As we breed a better killing machine of grace.

Within the didactic strategies of King Zombie
Great strides in the advancement of peace
Are bound to happen in waves and waves
Of glorious horde-like appetite fixations.

The legion marches on as the zombie troops
Ever closer strive to erase the stain of Man
From land and sea and everywhere else we can,
So sayeth we all, in one triumphant moan:

"Life is wasted on the living, so here we are.
We are the Dead and we shall surpass
All that Humanity has ever brought to bear
And as to Darwin, the Dead will trespass.

Against all manner of Human habitation
And throughout every level of isolation:
Humanity cannot hope to win against us
As in every way they are defenseless."

And the Institute of Higher Zombie Learning
Continues now and throughout the burning.
We never stop, nor wallow in useless fear
For it is the Cause alone that we hold dear.

The end is nigh; the Apocalypse is coming.
It's time you all were prepared for this event.
We are here to help you along on this path.
All you have to do is accept the Zombie wrath.

Please sign here, and here and here.
That's quite good, you see, my dear.
The nurse will show you to your room
And that's when we begin the Doom.

BED AND BREAKFAST
by
Joe Nazare

Reuben lies filling the king-sized bed and craving his namesake sandwich
(Just where on earth is his sister with today's groceries?)
When the local news cuts into *General Hospital* to document Armageddon:
A decadent horde roams the streets and makes a gory smorgasbord of the living.
Reuben watches it all with his jaws gaping and his jowls sagging,
Wondering if his spinster sister has *become* today's groceries.
Then either the televised horror or his lardy arteries stops his heart,
Transmuting his gross bundle of life into so much dead weight.

When a semblance of sentience returns, he feels an unprecedented hunger
Panging through his soulless carcass. His fresh appetites are
As outsized as he is; if he can only get up and trundle outside
Cannibalistic bliss awaits. He grunts and rocks yet remains
Turtled on his back, frustratingly resurrected, undead but bedridden.
He puddles drool on the coverlet, sees but one way out of this plush bear trap.
So showing more willpower than his static forerunner ever did, zombie Reuben
Presses a hammy arm to his maw and finally commits to reducing.

FEAST
by
J. Bradley

I chew on your lips,
Gnash them to fill the spaces
Between my teeth.

When other humans
Smell my breath, they will know
What it was like to kiss you.

I eat your cheeks,
Canvas the inside of my mouth
With them.

When I feast on the fingers of the living,
They will know what it was like
To caress your face.

I devour the back of your neck.
I always wanted to do this,
But at the time, I knew it'd kill you.

I chew on your wrists
Until your hands fall on the floor.

With my last ounce of humanity,
I pick them up, graft them into my hips
To forever walk with a piece of you.

Everyone will see
Your hands were tethers
When I was once filled with hydrogen.

I eat your stomach, spit it out
In remembrance of how much
You hated it sometimes.

I swallow your eyes whole
So you could always look at me.

These thoughts tempered
With the hope this doesn't happen,

That if the dead indeed roam the Earth
You would look at me one last time,
Say goodbye and punctuate it
With a shotgun shell to the head.

CRÈME BRÛLÉE
by Katherine Sanger

It's like custard,
She told me gleefully,
The first time
We scooped brains
Out of skulls
Together.

And even after
The food ran out
And I beat
Her to the punch
And scooped her
Brains out,

I still thought about
It.

CAROLINE

by
Eric Ian Steele

Sweet Caroline, you look at me
As if I was something to eat.
Saliva bubbles from your lips
Upon the floor they drip, drip, drip.

Not long ago I held you dear.
Now love is gone, replaced by fear
That if your wrists were not chained tight
I'd be the first to feel your bite.

In life your hair was coarse, spun gold,
Your lips the reddest crimson rose.
You never longed for company.
Now you simply moan and weep.

When you left me for that other
All my earthly joys were smothered.
So now you slowly rot and stink
For driving lovers to the brink.

Like a dog inside your cage
You gnash your teeth and scream with rage
Despite the fact you sit restrained
I feel your hatred and your pain.

Dear Caroline, how you despised
To even look me in the eyes,
Yet now the skin flakes from your head,
Tell me truly who is dead.

CANNED BEANS
by
Greg Schwartz

Canned beans again . . .
Outside, the zombies feast
On my neighbor.

INCARNATE
by
Jennifer Williams

Be still my beating heart
For you struggle so
You lead me to the empty streets
Where death lies in wait
Years pass
And I rise like a phoenix
To a changed world
Light no longer pollutes the skies
And stars are at the billions
My cold flesh knows no bounds
As I travel this Earth
I leave a trail of the dead
My breadcrumbs in the snow
And I have faith
In the emptiness of my soul

SAPID
by Adam J. Whitlatch

Your sweet meat soothes me
Live human flesh nourishes
Flesh of dog bitter

SLOW BITES
by Steve Vernon

Married at twenty.
A first child at twenty-three.
Two more before thirty.

Life gnawed at me,
The litany of job, wife, children,
Pieces of my well-being stolen away.

Rats in the walls
Nibble at my life with small insistent nips;
An inexorable extermination of existence.

Life nails our coffin with knocks on the door,
Weaving our gray-tainted obituary
One grocery receipt at a time.

Missed promotions,
Divorces and depression,
Death and devotion.

I haven't said it was painful.
The anaesthetic of just enough
Numbs the decay.

And now
As my wife and children
Feed greedily upon my limbs

I pray that as they
Work their way
To the slow gray jelly of memory

That they taste one savoured tang
Of the pleasure and tedium
That wore away my days.

IT'S NEVER TOO LATE
by
Roxanne Fuchs

There once was a zombie named Geoffrey,
Who by all means was a little too heavy;
People would say, "Oh what a sight!"
For he always took the biggest of bites.
His meals were plenty, but never good enough—
He would even complain the meat was too tough!
Until one day when he changed his mind,
And chose to leave his zombie days behind.

You may find it strange that a zombie could retire,
But this previous chef had a great desire
That all his meals had to taste great,
And this zombie's food was second rate.
So he changed his career,
Took off for a year,
And worked as an extra in movies.

PREPARING FOR THE EVENTUALITY
by
Stephen D. Rogers

My fever is spiking;
The wound,
It's not getting better.
How soon before it gets even worse?
How soon before I turn?
I'd been so careful,
But you can't prepare for every eventuality
Except perhaps
Death,
Returning from death,
Continuing after death.
I've seen what happens.
Of course
I was attacked.
I've seen what I'll become.
I try to accept that future.
I try not to judge.
I try to prepare for the eventuality.
I'm weaker,
Weaker by the moment and still
I want to reach my nerd friend before I turn.
My friend,
His brain,
It's got to be sweet.

THEM
by
Eric Ian Steele

Who is that
Shambling though the gravestones,
A tattered tuxedo hanging round his ankles?

What do they want,
Those shoppers in the empty mall,
Scrambling endlessly for the abandoned escalator?

Where are they going,
Those silhouettes who stumble
Through deserted streets at night?

How do they live,
Those ravaged faces that inhabit
The rat-infested city dump?

When will I hear
Their voices all around me
As I scream up at a dark and moonless sky?

THE END IS COME
by
Zombie Zak

The end is come.
Bitterness, betrayal, ill-gotten gains heaped upon disarray;
Denial, disgust, the breakdown of civilized communications,
A world in upheaval, an unwieldy time of dissent and dismay.
Communities crumble in the calamity that has ensued;
Rivers of death spew forth amongst the fallen hands of Man.
Chaos rules the streets while darkness watches on, laughing.
The end is come.

Distrust, fear, survival at any cost the only constant context.
Violence, brutality, social decay sets in and grips tightly
As the world burns while trying to dig itself out of its morass.
Paradigms shift, blending from Life affirmation to deadly reality,
Walking corpses shambling from out of every cavern and doorway,
Paving the way for the Hell on Earth that Mankind has unleashed.
The end is come.

Twisted, shambling, stunted combinations of decaying matter;
Rotted, fetid, empty husks of meat munching bags of splatter
Marching against the remaining, sad vestiges left in tatters.
Pockets of survivors gather and shiver in their hiding holes,
Fearful of the creeping doom that spirited away the light
Of freedom's hopes and dreams and crushed under dead foot.
The end is come.

Blood, meat, bones of the common Man strewn about the land,
Carcasses, revenants, the walking dead as one striding randomly
Across the face of what once used to be called a civilized world.
Cascades of pain and woe are all that remain of the human condition;
Misery flowing with zombie transmogrification, the dead are complete
And the time of Man slowly unwinds to something other than before.
The end is come.

A ZOMBIE SESTINA: ONLY FLESH
by
Tonia Brown

It's the last thing I remember, the taste of blood.
Which is odd, because it's what I woke to crave.
Well, that and the crunch of bone and tearing flesh
And the empty feeling of vast hunger, and this ache
Of being dead, of being undead, of simply death,
And dying at the hands of something strange.

I want to cry aloud, I feel so strange.
I cannot feel it run. (I mean my blood.)
I know that I am dead. I've seen my death,
And now I'm craving things I shouldn't crave
To fill and satisfy this horrid ache.
It all comes back to the need of flesh,

Or rather the need to feast on living flesh.
I cannot do it, yet I need to. Strange.
It's tearing me apart, this daunting ache.
I want to feel it run. (I mean my blood.)
I cannot focus beyond what I crave.
My memories are fading fast. Both life and death.

I can smell it now. I stink of death.
It smells so different from the fresh of flesh.
That scent only amplifies this crave.
I don't want to be this way, this strange.
If I could only feel it run, (I mean my blood)
Then I might imagine something else besides this ache.

Once I had a wife, now for her I ache,
Not to be her husband, but her death.
To make her run, and spill. (I mean her blood.)
To find out where she cowers. Smell her flesh?
I'm sure she'd find this new love of mine strange.
For once I wanted her, now her I truly crave.

For every single living thing I crave,
For every single hour grows this ache.
Funny thing, I no longer feel so strange.
I feel nothing now, but the rot of death,
And the urgent need brought on by flesh.
I need to feel it run. (I mean their blood.)

It might be strange to give into this crave.
But I know the taste of blood will ease the ache.
Now, I'm walking death and they are only flesh.

INVIDIA
by Jennifer Williams

I hunger
For a mouth that cannot feed
To be dead
Instead of undying
To be whole
And not decaying
I desire peace
In the earth beneath my feet
To sleep
A dreamless sleep
Pain is my companion
In this imitation of life
I envy
The living lost
The dwindling humanity
That they may cease to exist
Is my constant sorrow

SUCH A LITTLE THING
by
Camille Alexa

Charlie's funeral is nice,
As nice as such things go.
I cry and hold my daughter's hand
As she whimpers over Daddy,
Too young for my explanations.
A mutant bacterium is, after all,
Such a little thing.

It's dark.
Mourners have departed.
At the knock I wonder who forgot
Her casserole dish;
His keys;
His gloves;
Her scarf;
Or any of a thousand
Such little things.

I tuck my daughter into bed,
Descend the stairs,
Ignoring hairs rising on my neck,
A chill trickling down my spine
And deep in my chest,
Formless anticipation
Too intimate to define,
Like a single skipped beat of a heart:
Just a little thing.

Of course it's Charlie
Standing on our front stoop—
Or is it just my front stoop now?
Dozens of such inner queries

Shuffle inappropriately through my mind
As I stand before the husband I just buried.
The larger questions simply don't occur:
No, "How can you be here?"
No, "What's it like after death?"
Instead, it's, "May I throw out your razor?"
And, "How will I sleep at night without
Your weight next to mine?"
And other random, such stupid little things.

He gazes at me, mute, slack-jawed.
His eyes roll into his skull
Somewhere out of sight, just the whites
Glowing almost gently, two orbs
Without iris or pupil or rational thought.
A thin line of spittle wafts from his chin
On gentle nighttime breezes.
His best suit is splotched with mud;
His fingertips are ragged, nail-less:
Perhaps from clawing upward through
Mid-grade casket plywood?
It was the best I could afford,
And after Charlie was gone
—I thought forever—
Material concerns seemed
Such little things.

He thrusts his arms toward me,
A B-movie caricature of an undead thing;
Shuffles forward on nerveless stumps,
Rocks side to side with lurching gait,
Tonelessly groans and folds me in his arms,
Envelops me as though I was just
A tiny, little thing.

I freeze.
I breathe deep.
I draw into my lungs the acrid scent
Of formaldehyde, of starched funeral cotton.
Overriding the whiff of decay

Is a hint of earth and growing things.
I close my eyes and breathe again
Of him:
Father of my child,
Companion of my life,
The soft mineral salt scent of the man
I've slept beside for seven years.
To embrace him one last time
Is effortless,
Such a little thing.

He groans again
—Or is it a moan?—
And his arms spasmodically tighten.
His cheek near mine is rough as though
Unshaven; his chest does not rise and fall
With exhalation; he has no breath,
No heartbeat matching mine past
Layers of cloth and cloth and cloth.
His attention is wholly on me as it
Never was in life, his wettish smacking
In my ear gently tickling as it always did.
This small intimacy, soothingly familiar,
Lulls me as the smacking grows louder
And I smile dreamily, thinking my daughter
Will get one last farewell to her daddy.
That Charlie's love has always felt consuming
Seems all of a sudden a very little thing,
And after the first bite he takes
Such a very, very little thing indeed.

CORPSE, A HAIKU
by
Michael Cieslak

Rancid, flyblown flesh,
Putrefied, decomposing,
Moldering, yummy.

THEY EAT OUR BRAINS
by
J.C. Hay

They eat our brains but not our eyes,
And so from shelter I advise:
Hide in the first mall you come across
And do not dwell on true love's loss
Beneath the tide of zombies.

With shelter and food, please improvise
A weapon to hold what others prize,
And to defend your claims at any cost.
In times like this, all else is dross—
They eat our brains!

So if your love, covered o'er with flies,
Shouts words of love in groaning cries,
Recall he lies beneath the moss.
For should you let him in the house
You'll find where his true interest lies—
They eat our brains!

OH, SCHEHERAZADE
by
J.P. Wickwire

Oh, Scheherazade, what once we were
Beneath the willow tree.
The skies were blue, the water true,
And blades of grass were green.
Your voice then, o'er the fiddle,
And I, caught in the middle,
Wavering 'twixt love and rhapsody.

Oh, Scheherazade, with auburn hair,
With porcelain skin and face.
Your words of joy, both shy and coy;
Your eyelashes like lace.
The day they first came hither,
Freshly sown and withered,
You brushed his arm with naïve, foolish grace.

Oh, Scheherazade, your eyes did dim.
Your bones began to buckle.
It took you slow, I watched you go,
Fading, waning; subtle.
Your face turned ashen gray;
Your soul bent on decay.
Your wedding ring fell lifeless from your knuckle.

Oh, Scheherazade, I wept for you—
Was wont to rise at dawn,
Just to watch your lifeless limbs
Stumbling 'cross the lawn.
Our true love now mired.
My musket rests unfired.
How can I kill of which I am most fond?

Oh, Scheherazade, what shall I do
With dead men at my door?
I locked myself beneath the shelf
Of iron bars un-torn.
Are you among their numbers?
Do you tear me asunder?
Am I alone now and forevermore?

Oh, Scheherazade, my life's undone!
I shall not love another!
This rusty lock confines no more—
Throw open now, the shutters!
The moon above: snow-white.
I step into the night
To find you, love, amongst your undead brothers.

Oh, Scheherazade, the summer winds
Are besmirched by mindless moans.
You, though, shall be mine again.
Together we'll go home.
Death will quell my senses;
Love shattered my defenses.
My final wish: my hands for you to hold.

Oh, Scheherazade, what once we were,
Beneath the willow tree.
The sky now dead, the river's red
And still you come to me.
Sickness is my acquittal.
I die an empty riddle.
Still wavering 'twixt love and rhapsody.

SURVIVING THE HORDE
by
Peggy Christie

Whispers, quickly turning to sighs.
Low moans carry forward to my ears.
The wind blows my way and I
Smell them.
Rot. Decay. Death.
Gone, but they return.
Broken, but they move.
Dead, but they feed.
We are small in number now,
Hunted, prey. The living.
Scrabbling our survival in the dirt,
In the dark.
They have taken our place and we theirs.
When, why, and how are no longer important.
Dominance belongs to them even if they are unaware
Of their power.
Move, protect, hide, live. All that matters.
My scent on the wind and they redirect.
I can run, but not forever.
They have forever. They have all the time
In the world.

THE LIVING, THE DEAD, AND THE ENTROPIC

by
Eric Hermanson

They say it started with a Big Bang;
It ends with one as well.
The power outages, fires, and ashen skies
Followed with several months of Hell.

I tried to cling to my family,
Who from me were torn apart.
I ended up fleeing to the mountains
To forage a fresh new start.

The hills and foliage kiss the returning sun,
Life begins to push on again.
I hunt, I trap, I eat, I listen,
The cities can keep their festering undead.

A dead cowboy came into my camp last night
Obviously starving for living meat.
His decayed flesh sagged on his wiry bones;
I decapitated him after blowing off his feet.

My gunshots did not fall on deaf ears
For the next night there came two more:
A country bumpkin dripping dry crumbs,
A dead girl wearing an apron from the town store.

I put them down without much trouble,
But now I wonder if I should move on.
They're coming up from the flatlands in greater numbers,
Suburbanites even, with their dead family dogs.

So if you're living and reading this, please find me.
I fled higher once again where the air is thin.
It appears entropy takes a harder toll on dead flesh;
If we hold out long enough, we just might win.

THE WORLD HAS GONE TO HELL
by
Zombie Zak

The world has gone to Hell
And I don't feel all that well.

There where news reports and people talking tensely
All over the television and the radio and the Net.
The message they spread was one of the End Times.
Scared of all the worrisome ideas that I was seeing
I sought out my parents to find out what they thought.

The world has flipped its lid
And I don't know what they did.

The doorbell had rung its lilting singsong tone
To which my father rose from his chair to answer.
Not much more than a few seconds had past
When something rushed him, pushing him down.
Blood splattered everywhere and my world changed.

The world has cooked its goose
And I don't want to touch this noose.

In moments, they had filled the hall and living room.
At least five of the walking dead had entered our house;
Dad was fallen, and Mom I could not see her whereabouts.
I stayed quiet at the top of the stairs, as quiet as a mouse.
Screams soon followed as they all rushed to the kitchen.

The world has gotten whacked
And I don't see what's cracked.

I ran to my room and tried to block the door as best I could.
That would not matter; I was sure, as everybody was surely dead.
It was the end of all things that mattered, as far as I could tell.

Terror filled me and I was beside myself with what to do.
Awful noises crept up from downstairs and shambled about.

The world has popped its cork
And I don't want to end up like pork.

After much time had passed and silence seemed to rule,
I thought maybe now would be a good time to check things out.
The door opened without much fuss and not a single sound
As I creeped out into the hallway to quietly peek around.
Darkness, silence, grim and weary tick-tock noises were all I heard.

The world has faced its worst
And I think mankind was cursed.

It was a long time before I was comfortable getting down to the main floor.
Nothing moved except for Dad's grandfather clock in the living room.
It was then that I saw him against the wall, looking like a sack of meat.
I whimpered a little bit, seeing as everything was now dashed to pieces.
Wiping a tear away from my cheek, I noticed his head turn to face me.

The world has fallen down a hole
And I don't see much left of its soul.

It wasn't right, the way he now looked at me with eyes burning.
That was when I figured he had already become undead.
I turned to run away, but Mom had crept up right beside me.
She bit my arm as I plunged back up the stairs full tilt.
Pain burned through my limbs as I raced away from them.

The world has shot itself dead
And I don't like this dark dread.

Back to my room, all secure and fearful of the worst to come,
I knew full well I was now doomed the same as them.
But, at least I wanted my last few moments to be free of fear.
So I sat down and wrote this poem and posted it on the Web,
Hopeful that someday I would be remembered with peace.

The world has gone to Hell
And I don't feel all that well.

ESURIENT
by
Adam J. Whitlatch

I feel myself rot
Carrion birds peck my wounds
Your flesh calls to me

COLD, DEAD MEAT
by
C.A. Young

I like to keep him sluggish, store him in
A cool, dark place. Safe. Refrigerated.
Freshness sealed to stop him going rotten.
Once a day I throw him things I've butchered.

(I started to do that one afternoon
After I found a road-killed animal
On the side of the road, intestines strewn
Along the shoulder. Quite delectable.)

Blood-caked fingers and chin, he's like a child.
These days his eyes are pale and guileless, blind
To anything but cold, dead meat. Not riled
By things that are not food. He's tame. Confined.

It's not your fault you didn't understand.
I guess you'll get to see him eat firsthand.

ZOMBIE LOVE SONNET
by Anthony Watson

Biting deeply, fluids spurting, gushing.
Teeth that tear through tissue oh so sweet.
Time is pressing, still—no need for rushing.
Revel in the taste of fresh-killed meat.

Memories of real life no more than history,
Existence now a rush of blood, of lust.
Death has lost its sting, no more a mystery,
I go on while others turn to dust.

Your flesh is tender, succulent, sublime.
Your organs glisten in the morning light.
I know I loved you, once upon a time,
Your love for me a beacon in the night.
The bond that we now share is like no other—
I loved you then, I love you still, dear Mother.

WHEN THE DEAD WERE AMONG US
by
Kara Ferguson

Who knows how it began;
One can only guess.
A shower of meteorites, or
Military tampering gone awry?
A virus engineered for mass destruction?

Our family, friends and lovers rose
From their earthen beds.
It spread, devouring us all.
Insatiable hunger for the
Walking dead.
And we, the buffet, there
For the taking—complete devastation.

Frozen in shock, we struggled
To understand the invasion.
Highways flowed red with carnage
And mayhem.
Overrun and outnumbered.
We took shelter in basements
And old bomb shelters, and hoped for salvation.

The dead hunted and ate us.
Our modern world shutdown,
Unprepared, seeking refuge.
No nation remained standing.
Who would save us?

Little boys and young adults,
Well versed in science fiction.
The fact: it spread—the walking dead,
Devouring an established civilization.

They gathered up guns and sticks,
Crowbars and ammunition.
Science fiction? Present, fact.
We were saved by the video game,
Pop culture generation.

GIT ALONG, YOU ZOMBIES

by

Lester Smith

Git along, you zombies, from the main
cargo hold. The rocket is landed and I mean
to unload. It's your misfortune, not mine,
so git along. Nobody's gonna have to hear you moan
for brains, on the airless surface of the moon.

Nobody cares that you once had a name,
or that you once worked a pipeline in Nome.
You're all here now because you want to maim
living folks. So git along! In a vacuum you can mime
your hunger—till those "things" from Rigel Nine
come and eat you . . . . Though on Earth it's not well known,
this deal is what prevents an alien "High Noon."

TRAPPED
by
Sheri Gambino

What day is it, I'll always wonder?
Stuck so long in this damp bunker.
Am I the only person left alive?
I wait; will they get inside?
They came so fast and attacked,
Nothing we could do to react.
The things I saw will haunt me.
I have no future I can see.
You're wondering what are "they"—
Zombies, and I'm their prey.
I wait but they never leave;
Eating me is what they'll achieve.
Their moans are driving me mad.
No food or water left; I am sad.
Do I stay and starve to death,
Or go out and take my last breath?
I have finally made up my mind:
There is no escape from their kind.
I opened and walked out the door.
It was quick, I exist no more.

KISMET
by
Adam J. Whitlatch

The dead pound the door
Only have three bullets left
Save one for yourself

RAGE, RAGE IN THE DYING OF TWILIGHT
AFTER DYLAN THOMAS
by Rich Ristow

We must know the night is not that gentle—
in the distance, somebody new is screaming
long, hard, and anguished, only to stop abrupt.

It's intermittent and can drive the living mental,
questioning what's reality and what's dreaming.
We must know that the night is not gentle.

It rots and rises up from sewers. It is steaming
with microbes tunneling into flesh. It corrupts
every single brain cell. The infected are screaming,

while once-empty avenues seem poised to erupt
with decayed mobs baring teeth. They are resentful,
and though they stagger, they'll never stop abrupt.

This is not the time to be caught being sentimental,
eulogizing the recent dead. Murderers are seething,
and we must know this new night is not gentle—
every hour, somebody, in the distance, is screaming.

THE HUNGER
by
Susan Satterfield

Growling angry hunger
Ripping tattered remnants of lost souls
Swirling shattered memories
Flashing painful bursts of past life
Flowing in a river of blood and brain

Halting jarring movement
Stumbling steps toward nothing and everything
Passing through blasted human bastions
Hoping only for a drink—a taste
Pulsating from blood red rain

Rotting skin and muscle
Leaving ribbon trails of fetid flesh
Marking the path of desperate appetite
Wanting only nourishment—sustenance
Seeking shiny crimson fulfillment

Feeding without satisfaction
Finding only the emptiness of fearful famine
Rising forever through battered bone
Gnawing mindless agony fuels only
Growling angry hunger

THE WHITES OF THEIR EYES
by
Andrew J. Wilson

"Don't fire,"
He said,
"Till you see
The whites of their eyes."

So we waited,
Rifles cocked,
And waited,
Shivering in the cold,
Shuddering in fear.

The blizzard made everything white:
We could hardly make out
Anything at all
In the freshly-shaken snow globe
Our dugout had become.

But the whistling of the wind
Didn't drown out
The sounds
Of their creaking joints,
Or their endless snuffling.

Like truffle hounds,
Or Gadarene swine,
They tracked the subtle scent
Of the delicacies
Inside our skulls.

And then they were on us—
Our former comrades—
Hungry stick-men rearing
In our snow-blind faces.

"Sir!" someone screamed,
"They don't
Have
Any
Eyes . . ."

ZOMBIE WEATHER
by
Michael Kriesel

I'm mowing the old section of the cemetery.
Everything's in grainy black and white:
looks like zombie weather. I watch my back.
If there's just a couple, I'll run 'em over, raise
the mower deck and grind undead hamburger.
If more than two or three, this baby'll outrun
'em easy. If rotting corpses corner me over by
the tool shed, I'll swing a shovel at their heads
and run like crazy. I'm not spending half a reel
in jail, telling some fat cop they were dead
already. Soon he'll find out, and I'll be gone
so fast my name won't even make the credits.

BORN TO DEATH
by
Mark M. Johnson

Once warm and brimming with life
Now cold and devoid of the past
Up out of black empty nothingness
The comforting darkness of the void left behind
Sensations new and confusing
The unfamiliar weight of flesh encloses
Dead eyes open to blinding light
The new reality beckons
Empty no longer and filled with new purpose
Memories of nothing only need demanding
Searching for warmth and the life it must have
Relentless pursuit of its need
The living flee from the inevitable
Cornered prey fights for life in vain
Warm flesh in hand and the first sweet bite
Hot blood and living flesh
Cold rotting throat warmed with life
The need momentarily stilled
Its purpose is fulfilled

THE DAY OF RE-BIRTH
by
Sheri Gambino

It was a beautiful August day.
Everything was peaceful until it came.
Out of the sky dropped a glowing rock,
Hit the ground hard with a pop.
Thick green slime oozed everywhere,
Looking for a life form to ensnare.
Forming a small sludgy pond, waiting to be found;
From the heat of the travel it made a loud sizzling sound.

Young Timmy was nearby and saw a bright flash.
He took off to find the source with a dash.
Hearing the sizzle in the distance,
Moving forward with persistence,
Now finding the big blob of slime,
Advancing towards this incredible find.
Lowering his hand into the mass of slime,
It jumped and entered him in practically no time.
His mouth and nose burnt like hell,
Screaming in pain he tried to run but fell.
Green slime burned him inside and out;
His mouth so swollen he could not shout.
Starting to shake and convulse,
His eyes rolled back, he had no pulse.

The life form coursed through his blood.
Skin turned green and became bloated.
His eyes opened, looking around.
Pulling himself off the ground,
Green froth dripping down his chin;
Now to find food to eat, he grinned.
Quickly, he found a small town.
Started running and chasing people down.

Biting, tearing, eating them alive,
Making him stronger, he started to thrive.
People laid dead everywhere on the street,
Defeated by a zombie virus packaged so petite.
His bites brought them back to life.
They were rabid and ready for strife.
Timmy looked at his undead army.
They followed him all green and slimy.
He told them, "Time to take over the Earth."
Everyone would take part in his undead re-birth.

MORTE D'AMOUR
by Jennifer Williams

No Spark
In my lover's eyes
Hunger only, staring out
Insatiable
No warmth
In his flesh upon my flesh
Diseased and cold and hanging by a thread
No soul
Because my love is dead
Dead and clinging with desire
Roses, rotting
Spill from his mouth
In our mock embrace
And I think his heart beats once
Within its bone-white cage
As my last breath
Whispers his name

HEAD OUT
by
Nathalie Boisard-Beudin

There was a complaint.
A bony finger lifted.
"Way too many thoughts"—
Too many thoughts in a brain
Make it difficult to chew.

"I like memories,"
She said—coyly—head tilted,
Dark orbits blinking.
"They are sweet, smooth on the tongue,
But thoughts get between my teeth."

The head waiter blushed,
Frowning over the dish at
The offending brains
Openly gritty with knowledge,
Congealed among the juices.

Apologies bloomed:
Adult minds could be so tough—
Unpredictable—
You never knew where they'd been
Or what they were built around.

New cerebellum.
"Infant, perhaps?" was proposed.
A replacement dish
For a trusted customer
Disgusted by gray matter.

She was most sorry,
But baby brains were no good.

No flavour to them
"You see? Just the opposite . . ."
No experience, no taste.

She needed a treat,
Our head waiter did agree.
A new plate was brought,
Bearing his own brains on it
For customers must come first.

She was delighted:
Service in this restaurant
Was indeed superb.
It was in all the guide books,
And well worth a three heads mark.

ZOMBIE SEMI-SONNET
by J.H. Hobson

Bad. Feel bad. Not full. Need
Brains. Must find brains. Eat Brains!
Warm gray matter. Sustains
Me. Look. A street. Streets lead
To the brains. Mmmmm. Brains! Smell
The brains. So close! Reach arm
Out. Catch all those brains. Warm
Gushy brains. Sweet. Feel well.
Good. Brains. Look. More people
Coming. Mmmmm. New brains. Uh huh!
Brains! I will eat all the
New brains . . . . Oh no, they pull
Out blades. Sharp! Head hits floor.
No . . . more . . . brains . . . any . . . more . . .

FRED

by
Berrien C. Henderson

There once was a zombie named Fred
Who was an atypical undead.
Whenever his friends ate
Brains and entrails at plate
He'd say, "Gimme some greens instead."

DEVOLVEMENT
by
Ginger Nielsen

A whisper, a sigh, eyes hollowed and mouth agape,
Her skeletal arms outstretched, strewn with decomposing flesh,
She beckons to you, she needs you, she can smell you.
Her blonde hair matted and clotted with filth, her gown shredded and soiled,
She shambles, she staggers, her lidless eyes watching your every move.
You flee, you hide, but she will always find you, inexhaustible in her efforts
And if you give in, what then? The end of life, an undead resurrection?
To have her teeth crush into your skull, to be confined in her frigid embrace,
Is certainly a fate worse than death.
Thereupon, you would be condemned to kill, an insatiable hunger for others,
Craving the feeling of warm flesh and blood, the brains within their skulls.
She's closer still, and she moves with renewed anticipation.
A guttural moan emits from torn and crusted lips as she grasps at you
And you have become so weary of running, of hiding,
This unending struggle to survive in an already-dead world.
There are no more bullets, no more blades;
Your arms are weak and your legs finally give in.
You can almost see the desire in her milky eyes as her mouth widens.
You feel her cold and spoiled flesh against yours, biting through your skull.
And now, you are one of the same,
Dead but still existing, rotting but still remaining.
Craving the flesh of those unfortunates still alive and hiding,
Hiding from you.

DEADLY RELATIONSHIPS
by
Patsy Collins

When you're a zombie, you must keep your cool.
Just keep your head, once you're the undead.
A bokor called you back, so you're his to rule.
Your thoughts always led by the things he said;
Wish to be dead.

No blood in your veins now, just bokor's drugs.
No thoughts in your mind, neither cruel nor kind.
You'll be bokor's nursemaid or one of his thugs.
To him confined, life and death combined,
No role defined.

Who'd ever know that inside the slave,
Once was a lover, wife and a mother,
Who gave up the freedom you now crave.
I took poisoned puffer, so that another
Wouldn't suffer.

Zombies never sleep and zombies never dream,
Unable to pray for there's nothing to say.
Can't release your anger in a silent scream;
Just wait for the day that you rot away.
Total decay.

So now I must wait for my child to grow;
Watch bokor feed, what grew from his seed.
Find a way, the truth to let his boy know,
So he'll find the need, to overcome bokor's greed;
See me freed.

It's your life I saved, my darling son.
Mine you must take, make no mistake,

Only with my death, can the spell be undone.
Use bullet and stake, betony and mandrake.
I must never wake.

ZOMBIE ATTACK ESCAPE PLAN
by
Claire Askew

While most people plan
For fire and flood, earthquakes,
Winters, acts of God,

You plot a course
For the day
Someone meddles—

The day
Some new Frankenstein
Raises the dead.

It'll come, you're convinced—
While others stack tins
In hurricane cellars,

Fill sandbags for ice-melt,
And you're out in the graveyard
Writing down names.

You've read how long
The brain takes to decay
(Without brains

They're harmless)—
So catalogue and file
Only the fresh ones.

It's no coincidence
You live on the fifth floor,
Two doors

From the hunt shop,
Its stockpile of shotguns,
Ammo and knives.

You figure it'll take a while
Before they claw themselves
Out of the earth—

Your first plan is defence.
Eventually, some doctor
Will invent the antidote,

Then you'll attack.
Last, if all other plans
Fail, there's logic:

You feel confident
You could negotiate them
Back to the grave.

My own plan is secret.
I'm sure I'm no match
For the thirsty undead,

Weak, afraid, too filled up
With blood—I'd lie down in the dark,
Wait to be bitten.

PAYBACK TIME
by
Paul A. Freeman

The nations of the world were horrified
To find their populations zombified.
Yet whilst the deadly virus quickly spread
Across the globe, I lounged in bed
And sulked as only teenage boys can do.
For as the threat of the Zombie Virus grew,
My parents wouldn't let me have some fun
With ax, or spade, or Daddy's gun.
Instead they left me home and drove the car
Down to the local mall (which wasn't far)
To fetch provisions so we wouldn't lack
Necessities—yet neither one came back.

My chance had come, and so I ventured out
Armed to the teeth, indulging in a bout
Of vengeance 'gainst my neighbors, now undead,
Who used to call me loutish and ill-bred.
Then suddenly my mom and dad turned up,
As zombies, on my flesh intent to sup!
Dim memories had drawn them to our house—
Their thirst for blood I felt obliged to douse.

For grounding me I used a spade to cull
My dear papa, and cleaved in two his skull.
And as for Mom, who often made me sick
By feeding me green vegetables, a stick
Was what I used to beat her head until
From nose and ears her brains had spilled.

What jolly fun! thought I, and moseyed down
On foot towards the centre of the town.
Amongst the carnage, looking rather glum,

With sword in hand and chewing on gum
Sat Kelly Klein, a classmate from my school,
Who hadn't yet been changed into a ghoul.
On seeing me, she ran to my embrace
And hugged me hard, though up till now my face
Had not been one deemed worthy of a friend.
"The world we know is coming to an end,"
She cried, whilst in a clinch she held me tight.
"Against these undead legions we must fight."

The words she spoke were music to my ears,
For in my mind I now replayed the jeers
Of everyone who'd ever called me "geek,"
Or branded me a "dumb-ass," "creep" or "freak."
Upon those schoolyard cliques I'd be revenged,
For every cruel jest I'd be avenged.

"These zombies seek out places that they know,"
I told my newfound ally, "so let's go
To Hayward High where colleagues who have turned
To ghouls can be impaled, or stabbed, or burned.
For surely school's the place they know the best,
And that's where we shall put them all to rest."

But first we cleared the road of living dead,
With ax and sword, till many were heads
Upon the sidewalk lying at our feet
Or rolling down the carcass-littered street.

Then once our brutal duty was fulfilled,
We left the downtown district where we'd spilled
A sea of blood and strode to Hayward High,
To bid a final, violence-fuelled goodbye
To those who'd made my life at school a hell,
By chopping up each shuffling, corpse-like shell.

For Kelly, too, the journey was a quest,
Since girls are known for bullying with zest,
And often she was victim of a joke
That made her sniff or tearfully to choke.

The football field was where we ventured first,
As sportsmen are undoubtedly the worst
For meanness and for cruelty *per se*.
These jocks, who once like donkeys used to bray
Their insults now trudged dumbly 'cross the ground,
Whilst majorettes marched woodenly around
To old routines they seemed to recollect.
"It's time to teach these evil cows respect,"
Cried Kelly as she set about the band
Of majorettes, her sword gripped in hand.
Methodically she severed all their limbs
Before the killer blow whilst humming hymns
She'd learned in childhood sitting in the pews.
And in the meantime I got ready to abuse
Those athletes who'd condemned me as a nerd.
The first I downed was Jimmy Jones the Third,
A quarterback who'd nicknamed me "The Worm,"
Whose daddy owned a rich commercial firm.
With glee I swung my lumber cutter's ax
Between his eyes, then countered the attacks
Of loping members of his football team.
But soon the interjection of a scream
Curtailed my bloody fun, for Kelly's arm
Was grasped by one intent on mortal harm.

A zombie majorette had sneaked behind
My classmate hoping such a ploy would find
The girl caught unawares and easy prey.
Alas, poor Kelly seemed about to pay
A dreadful price for letting down her guard
Until her foot drew back and gave a hard
Uncompromising kick that left the ghoul
Upon her back. Then Kelly raised her tool
Of steely death and diced the majorette.
Yet as she hacked away I had to fret,
For though her undead sister was dispatched,
It looked like Kelly's forearm had been scratched.

"Let's hurry to the changing rooms, right now,"

Said I, "and if this wound's your final bow,
So be it—though an antiseptic cream
Applied with haste might keep alive the dream
I'm nurturing that side-by-side we'll fight
To end the menace of this gruesome blight."

She stroked my cheek, then sprinted like a fox
To show me where we'd find the first aid box
Inside a changing room, upon the wall.
"Together, killing fiends, we'll have a ball,"
Said Kelly, as I took her injured arm
And smothered on the wound a soothing balm.

An hour passed, yet still she looked unchanged;
No foaming at the mouth, nor words deranged.
Since neither blood nor human flesh she craved,
It seemed that by prompt action she'd been saved.

"My hero!" Kelly purred in my ear,
Relieving from my soul the nagging fear
That soon a swift removal of her head
Was needed to ensure her staying dead.

Then heaven! Kelly clamped her lips on mine.
So this is love, thought I, as down my spine
A tingling passed of utter teenage bliss.
Yet when we disentangled from our kiss
It felt as though my mouth had just been stung
By bees until I spied my severed tongue
Twixt Kelly's lips and bloodlust in her eyes.
And as I tried to grasp this grim surprise,
My former schoolmates battered down the door
Whilst Kelly forced me screaming to the floor
Where weight of biting numbers brought a flood
Upon the ground of bright arterial blood.

Now though I'm kind of dead, it's not the end,
For Kelly's now my soul-mate and my friend.
Our love is strong, yet hunger's stronger still,
Which forces us to torture, maim and kill.

So if you see us in your town one day,
Just pray we don't come shuffling your way.

Blood of the Dead, a hard-hitting, shoot 'em up zombie novel. The Haven was once a sanctuary in a world filled with the undead. Now the zombies are on the move and Joe Bailey must leave the Haven, dragging two others along with him, and go to the one place all fear to tread: the heart of the city. Walking corpses reign in this hardcore tale of zombies, blood and bullets.

Available at Amazon.com - Barnesandnoble.com - 978-1-897217-80-1

38 authors. 38 stories. Featuring deadly tales of zombies from the likes of Piers Anthony, Nancy Kilpatrick, Jeff Strand, Michael Laimo, Nick Cato, Steven Savile, Gina Ranalli and many more . . .
Bits of the Dead is a hard-hitting, pulse-pounding collection of zombie tales that'll have you ripping through the pages faster than a ghoul through a warm body.

Available at Amazon.com - Barnesandnoble.com - 978-1-897217-81-8

A missing boy. A lone hero. A whole lot of zombies. A black cloud that takes Axiom-man to a world not his own. A dead world, where a gray and brown sky shrouds an entire city in a miasma of decay. The streets are empty. The young boy is nowhere to be found. Those he does find . . . are dead. And walking.

Axiom-man: The Dead Land

Available at Amazon.com - Barnesandnoble.com - 978-1-897217-83-2

Science. Research. Knowledge. The human intellect knows no bounds because of them. Sometimes . . . science goes wrong.
Death. Destruction. Zombies. Featuring the terrifying tales of 13 authors, *Dead Science* brings you stories of the undead unlike any you've ever read before.

Available at Amazon.com - Barnesandnoble.com - 978-1-897217-85-6

Times are tough. The dead have risen up to feast on the living. Zora, an army deserter who hears voices from above, joins up with a baldly scalded nuke-survivor named Zeno in order to locate Ahura Mazda and deliver a taste of justice to the cowards who orchestrated the apocalypse . . . preferably without being served up as zombie lunch-meat.
Zombifrieze: Barnacles

Available at Amazon.com - Barnesandnoble.com - 978-1-897217-93-1

Chev Worke thought he had found a path to easy money. He just didn't count on things going wrong and getting stranded on State Highway 59 with no one around except for a pack of hungry werewolves. Chev makes it to a grocery store in Easter Glen only to learn of a secret pact that has been in place for centuries. There's just one problem: the pact has been broken.

Available at Amazon.com - Barnesandnoble.com - 978-1-897217-87-0

Where Imagination is Truth

www.coscomentertainment.com

Two mob families go to war and the current Don is buried alive on a construction site that was once the location of a church that had banned the same Don's ancestors. Major problems arise when a group of mysterious Sicilians arrive and manage to retrieve the Don's corpse. Well, his *living* corpse. Before long, the Don's undead state leads to the outbreak of reanimated dead. Capisce? *Don of the Dead.*

Available at Amazon.com - Barnesandnoble.com - 978-1-926712-03-1

The invasion begins and the dead start to rise. There's panic in the streets of London as invaders from Mars wreak havoc on the living. But that's not the only struggle mankind must face. The dead are rising from their graves with an insatiable hunger for human flesh. It's kill or be killed, otherwise you might become one of the walking dead yourself.

The War of the Worlds Plus Blood, Guts and Zombies

Available at Amazon.com - Barnesandnoble.com - 978-1-897217-91-7

This ain't your grandfather's Huckleberry Finn. A mutant strain of tuberculosis is bringing its victims back from the dead. In this revised take on history and classic literature, the modern age is ending before it ever begins. Huckleberry Finn will inherit a world of horror and death, and he knows the mighty Mississippi might be the only way out . . .

Adventures of Huckleberry Finn and Zombie Jim

Available at Amazon.com - Barnesandnoble.com - 978-1-897217-97-9

AVAILABLE FROM LIBRARY OF THE LIVING DEAD PRESS

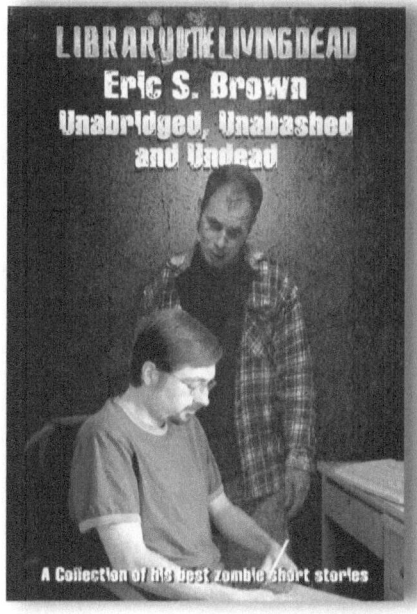

AND COMING SOON:
ZOMBOLOGY
A HUGE TOME OF UNDEAD SHORT STORIES

www.ingramcontent.com/pod-product-compliance
Lightning Source LLC
Chambersburg PA
CBHW021110080526
44587CB00010B/470